Remembrance

GURUMAYI CHIDVILASANANDA

Remembrance

GURUMAYI CHIDVILASANANDA

PUBLISHED BY SYDA FOUNDATION
A SIDDHA YOGA MEDITATION PUBLICATION

Remembrance

Practice remembrance ~

remembering the Lord, remembering grace,

remembering the goodness people have offered you.

Remember your own great experiences.

Remember your own heart.

This is the way to moksha, liberation.

GURUMAYI CHIDVILASANANDA

Published by SYDA Foundation
371 Brickman Rd., P.O. Box 600, South Fallsburg, New York 12779, USA

Cover photograph by Luis Barrios

Acknowledgments

*This volume came into being through the loving service of many dedicated and talented people: Valerie Sensabaugh,
the managing editor; Cheryl Crawford, the designer; Sushila Traverse and Osnat Shurer, who oversaw production;
Hans-Georg Tuerstig, the Sanskrit advisor; Leesa Stanion, who compiled the index; the tireless members of the
SYDA Documentation Department; and many others who made unique and valuable contributions.
We offer grateful thanks to each one.*

Kshama Ferrar and Sarah Scott

Printed in the United States of America

First edition 1998
05 04 03 02 01 00 99 98   5 4 3 2 1

Library of Congress Cataloging-in-Publication Data
Chidvilasananda, Gurumayi.
    Remembrance/Gurumayi Chidvilasananda
        p. cm.
    Includes bibliographical references and index.
    ISBN 0-911307-63-X (pbk. : alk. paper)
    I. Spiritual life—Hinduism.   I. Title.
BL1238.32.C44   1998
294.5'44—DC21   98-18494
                                CIP

Copyright permissions appear on page 74.

Printed on recycled paper that meets the minimum requirements
of the American National Standard for Information Sciences.

Contents

Preface

As human beings, we remember so many things. We remember our happy times and also times of sorrow. We remember our worthy actions and actions that brought regret. We remember our loved ones and even strangers who in a passing moment showed us something about life. We just cannot live without remembering. Since this is the case, why not remember the things that uplift us, that allow us to contribute our best to the world?

In this inspired collection of informal talks, Gurumayi Chidvilasananda draws our attention to the great things in our lives that are worth remembering. She reminds us of our own innate goodness, of our worthiness to give and receive love, of the extraordinary blessings that flow through our lives like joyous streams rushing toward the ocean in spring-time. This book is like a *japa mālā*, a set of rosary beads. It holds the power of remembrance for what is beautiful and sacred in our lives.

People say that when they inhale the fragrance of jasmine flowers, it transports them to a beautiful realm, a place like Gurudev Siddha Peeth, the mother ashram of Siddha Yoga meditation. There in the abundant gardens, the scent of jasmine fills the air with its intoxication. This book is like that. It transports us to remembrance of the highest.

The talks in this collection were given during the Siddha Yoga meditation retreat at Shree Muktananda Ashram in the summer of 1997. The first two talks are from the Guru Purnima weekend, the time of the full moon in July, when the supreme principle of grace, the Guru, is honored. The third talk was given on Rakhi Day, the day of protection celebrated during the full moon in August. The final talk, given on the new moon of September, honors the fiftieth anniversary of Swami Muktananda's *divya dīkshā*, the day he was initiated by his Guru, Bhagawan Nityananda.

Many, many people who were present in the Shakti Mandap, the great hall of Shree Muktananda Ashram, when Gurumayi gave these talks have asked that they be published. Many others who heard about them have expressed the same yearning. To honor these requests, and on behalf of readers who are meeting these words for the first time, we are extremely happy to be able to make such historic talks available in printed form. They have already changed many lives for the better and will surely continue to do so. May you receive from these words, each time you read them, exactly what you need.

Kshama Ferrar and Sarah Scott, Editors
Shree Muktananda Ashram
May, 1998

Guru Purnima

Guru Purnima

Chapter 1

My Heart Delights in My Sadguru

With great respect, with great love, I welcome you all with all my heart.

The moon is very full now, and in a few minutes it will be at the peak of its fullness. Happy Guru Purnima!

On Guru Purnima, the fullest moon of the year, we offer salutations to the primordial Guru, Lord Shiva. We honor the lineage of great Masters who bestow shaktipat and awaken the dormant *kundalinī* energy within. Guru Purnima is a time we celebrate the Siddhas of this great lineage. We live because of their blessings. We die because of their blessings. Let us remember our gratitude, our love, every moment of our lives. We owe our existence to such great souls.

Once Baba Muktananda was answering a seeker's question about the true nature of the Guru. "When I first met you," the man said, "you were in my thoughts constantly. Now it seems that your presence in my mind has become more subtle. Is this true or is it my imagination?"

Baba said, "This is a sign of great progress! I will become more and more subtle and then merge with you. No matter what you do in your daily life . . . keep reminding yourself that you are a portion of supreme Consciousness, which lives in its fullness inside you. . . . Cultivate this awareness over and over again. . . .

"Keep worshiping your Self every day with great honor. The sacred water is inside you; it will cleanse you."

Baba's answer is so beautiful and profound. "The sacred water is inside you; it will cleanse you." Who is it that makes us become aware of this sacred water, this life-giving nectar within us? Who is it that uncovers the light that illumines our lives? It is the Guru—the Guru's grace and blessings. Having awakened our knowledge about the sacred water inside ourselves, the Guru also guides us.

And what is this "sacred water"? It is supreme knowledge. It is the love of the heart. It is ecstasy, supreme bliss. It is seeing God in this universe. The sacred water represents different things for different seekers depending on their maturity on the path, depending on the depth of their sadhana.

The great poet-saint Kabir spoke about the sacred water as true love. In one of his poems, he sang:

O sadhus, O noble-hearted people,
my heart delights in my Sadguru.
He fills the cup of true love again and again.
He drinks from it himself and also offers it to me.
O sadhus, O noble-hearted people,
my heart delights in my Sadguru.

Baba Muktananda used to sing the poems of Kabir with great delight because they expressed his own experience so beautifully. In his spiritual autobiography, *Play of Consciousness,* Baba praises his Sadguru, Bhagawan Nityananda, saying:

> How can we sing the greatness of such a Guru? Nityananda is everything to Muktananda. His supreme father, his deity, his ecstasy, his meditation, and his *samādhi* are solely Nityananda, beloved Nityananda. "I worship the Sadguru, the beloved Guru"— singing thus, can I ever repay your bounty? No, Gurudev. You are almighty.

The Full Moon of the Guru

Guru Purnima. The full moon of the Guru. Baba says, "The sacred water is inside you, it will cleanse you." Kabir says, "O sadhus, O noble-hearted people, my heart delights in my Sadguru." And the English poet John Keats asks:

> What is there in thee, Moon,
> that thou should'st move my heart so potently?

"What is there in thee, Moon?" When your heart is open and you see the moon, you are enchanted by her fullness, by her light. The sacred water inside you is drawn to the fullness of the moon. The sacred water inside you draws the moon into yourself. You forget which is the moon: the moon in the sky or the moon in your very being.

In the *Bhagavad Gītā*, the Lord speaks about the subtle nature of the moon:

> Among all the heavenly bodies, I am the moon.
> Permeating the earth, I sustain all beings
> with My strength,
> and as *soma*, liquid moonlight,
> I help all healing plants to flourish.

"Among all the heavenly bodies, I am the moon," says the Lord. No wonder the moon moves our hearts so potently! The Lord Himself is the moon, so it is He who steals our hearts.

"Permeating the earth, I sustain all beings with My strength," explains Lord Krishna. He is telling us He is the strength. Isn't that a great discovery? You don't have to work so hard anymore! You just have to think of the Lord, and you have all the strength you need. It's true! You can experience it for yourself.

"As *soma*, liquid moonlight, I help all healing plants to flourish," the Lord says. In India, it is said that if you are not feeling well and you gaze at the moon for some time each night, or if you allow the rays of the moon to fall upon you, then you experience the healing energy of the moonlight, the liquid moonlight.

Jnaneshwar Maharaj, commenting on this verse of the *Bhagavad Gītā*, says:

> O Arjuna,
> I am the moon, a moving lake of nectar in the sky.
> With moonbeams pouring down in limitless streams,
> I nourish all vegetation.
> In this way, crops of all kinds are produced
> that give food to every living creature.
> I am the moon, a moving lake of nectar in the sky.

A Moving Lake of Nectar

Last night after I had gone to bed, I could not fall asleep. As I lay there, I realized the little pillow under my head was wet. Wonderful tears of gratitude for the Guru were flowing down my face. As I touched the tears, I recognized that my heart was remembering Baba. My heart was picturing him: his eyes, his hands, his words, his movements, his energy, his presence. I realized that soon the moon would be very full and I wondered if it was visible.

I got up and went outside. It was glorious. The stars were shining brilliantly. White clouds and dark stormy clouds were moving gently in the sky, and the moon was cradled in these clouds. It was drizzling and cool. I *pranāmed* to the moon, the

Guru Purnima moon, the full moon. I call it the Baba moon. In May, on Baba's birthday, I also call that full moon the Baba moon. And again in October, at Baba's *mahāsamādhi*, I call the full moon the Baba moon. Three full moons, three Baba moons. But then last night I realized that every day there is a full moon. Liquid moonlight is always streaming into our hearts and from our hearts into the universe.

It was a glorious evening. I kept watching the moon. It revealed a fiery ring, and then at times it would be hidden behind the clouds. Jnaneshwar Maharaj's words, "a moving lake of nectar in the sky," kept resounding in my being. I wanted to touch the moon. I wanted the moon to touch me. I wanted the moon to bestow her blessings upon the entire universe. I knew many thousands of devotees were also watching the same moon, beholding her glory, her beauty. "O Arjuna, I am the moon, a moving lake of nectar in the sky."

In the Indian scriptures, the moon has many names and descriptions. In fact, there is an ancient hymn containing twenty-eight different names for the moon. These names are very beautiful and they evoke something that you feel but cannot always articulate. The Luminous One, the Drop of Soma, the Maker of Night, the Lord of Constellations, the One with Cool White Rays, the Maker of Nectar. That's how it was last night when I went to the Temple. The moon was pure white, like nectar.

There are many more names. The Crown of Shiva, Marked Like a Deer, the Lord of the Lotus. Can't you just imagine the moonlight and the smile of the night-blooming lotus as it opens in the liquid rays of moonlight? Think of your own heart when sadhana seems very, very dark—and then you see the moonlight, the Lord of the Lotus. What happens to your heart then?

Another name for the moon is Drawn by White Horses. Last night the moon looked like that. The white clouds were like horses drawing the moon. Sometimes the clouds looked like a lake, and then the moon was a moving lake of nectar in the sky.

As one writer has said, "The moon is the vessel of divine ambrosia drunk by the ancestors and the gods, yet ever refilled again." The moon is so enchanting.

Seeing Him I See Everything

Baba says, "The sacred water is inside you. It will cleanse you." Kabir sings, "O sadhus, my heart delights in my Sadguru." And the Sufi poet Hafiz says:

> The moon is most happy
> When it is full.
>
> And the sun always looks
> Like a perfectly minted gold coin

That was just Polished
And placed in flight
By God's playful Kiss.

And so many varieties of fruit
Hang plump and round

From branches that seem like a Sculptor's hands.

I see the beautiful curve of a pregnant belly
Shaped by a soul within,

And the Earth itself,
And the planets and the Spheres—

I have gotten the hint:

There is something about circles
The Beloved likes.

Hafiz,
Within the Circle of a Perfect One

There is an Infinite Community
Of Light.

Relish these words, delight in them. "Within the Circle of a Perfect One there is an Infinite Community of Light." Within the circle of a perfect one, there is infinite grace.

One of Baba's favorite quotes from the philosophy of Kashmir Shaivism was *gururvā pārameshvarī anugrāhikā shaktih,* "The Guru is the grace-bestowing power of God." This recognition is what Kabir is describing when he says:

O sadhus, my heart delights in my Sadguru.
He fills the cup of true love again and again.
He drinks from it himself and also offers it to me.

He removes the veil from my eyes
and gives me the true vision of God.

Seeing him, I see everything.
He enables me to hear the eternal sound
of the unstruck music resounding in my heart.

He shows joy and sorrow to be one and the same.
By giving me the Word, he fills me
with the ecstasy of divine union.

Kabir says,
Truly, that person has no dread nor anguish
upon whom the Guru has bestowed fearlessness.

O sadhus, O noble-hearted people,
my heart delights in my Sadguru.
Seeing him, I see everything.

Who Attains Fullness?

Once there was a great Guru named Agnishiva who had four
wonderful disciples. When the time came for him to take
mahāsamādhi, to leave his physical body and merge into
supreme Shiva completely, he called the four disciples. "I must
leave my physical body," he said. " I want to give you all my
power and all my knowledge, all my shakti and all my grace."
To one of the disciples, he gave a dry chapati. (A chapati is a

flat bread commonly served in India.) To the second disciple, he gave his own blanket. To the third disciple, he gave his own mound of *vibhūti*, the sacred ash he applied on his body while he meditated. And then he realized he did not have anything to give to the fourth disciple. He looked around for something to give.

As I was reading this story, it reminded me of Baba. Sometimes he would call people to give them *prasād*. "Come," he would say. "There is *prasād* here. I want to give you something." And he would start giving. Then he would realize there was not enough for everyone. But Baba was a generous Guru. He was not going to say, "Sorry folks, we've run out." No. He would look around. And sometimes he would notice one of his disciples who was wearing a shawl, and he would say, "You don't need that shawl, do you?" And the disciple . . . well, I don't need to describe the details of what the disciple would go through. Of course, later Baba would give something infinitely glorious to the person who had given up his shawl.

Like Baba, Agnishiva did find something to give—he remembered his old shoes. "Here's something," he said, and he gave the fourth disciple a pair of his shoes.

Now, who attained Self-realization? Who attained everything? Can you guess?

You might think it was the one who received the shoes. Well, let me clarify. When each one received his *prasād* from the Guru, he didn't even look at the object. He remembered only what the Guru had said: "I want to give you all my power, all my knowledge. I want to give you all my grace and all my shakti." That message was resounding fully in the hearts of the four disciples. The object that had been given didn't really matter. They did not judge. They did not wonder. They did not think, "Agnishiva likes him better than me. I always knew he favored him." No. None of that was going through their minds. The dry chapati was ambrosia. The blanket was ambrosia. The mound of ash was ambrosia. The old shoes were ambrosia. They had each received ambrosia, liquid moonlight streaming from the hands of their Sadguru. And that is what they attained. Each of them attained fullness.

This is why Kabir sings:

O sadhus, my heart delights in my Sadguru.
Any impurity in my perception, he removes it.
By removing the impurity in my understanding,
he gives me the darshan of the Supreme.
He makes me taste God.
He makes me touch God.
He makes me hear God's voice,
the unstruck sound in my heart.
My heart sings, sings his glory.

Joy and Sorrow Are the Same

Guru Purnima, the full moon of the Guru. Why do people worship the full moon? Because she makes you feel full in your heart. She fills you with God's love. She says, "Look at me. I wax and wane. Do I ever lose my happiness? Do I ever lose my true luster?"

As Kabir sings:

> O sadhus, my heart delights in my Sadguru.
> He fills the cup of true love again and again.
> He drinks from it himself and offers it to me.
> O sadhus, my heart delights in my Sadguru.
> He gives me the teaching
> that joy and sorrow are the same.

Joy and sorrow are the same, says Kabir. One day you are happy, the next day you are remorseful; they are the same. One day you feel great, another day you feel bad; they are the same. There is no difference, says Kabir. My Guru shows me that joy and sorrow are the same.

Just because you are happy or unhappy you don't have to gain weight or lose weight. You don't have to throw away your steadiness. You should know where strength comes from, and you should know who receives the fruit of that strength. The strength comes from God. Liquid moonlight streams into everyone's life making you healthy and strong, purifying your understanding. As the Lord says, With My strength I nourish this entire universe.

It Is Time to Attain Wisdom

Once in the golden age of Greece, there was a great seeker. He was studying under a Master who had a unique way of giving instructions. The Master would give one teaching that the seeker would follow for a long time. He did not give lengthy talks or hold daily satsangs. He gave just one teaching at a time.

One day the Master told this seeker, "Every time someone insults you, give him some money." Now even though this man was a great seeker, he did make mistakes from time to time, and there were people in that town who insulted him. So over time he paid out quite a bit of money. After three years he met his teacher once again. "How long have you been paying people who insult you?" asked the Master.

"A long time," sighed the disciple. "Three years, twelve days, and one hour."

"Very good," said the Master. And then he gave a new instruction. "Now it is time for you to attain wisdom. Go to Athens and there you'll meet someone."

When the disciple reached Athens, he met a certain wise being who sat at the gates of the city insulting everyone who came and went. Right away he began to insult this newcomer. And immediately, the disciple burst into laughter.

"Sit down," said the wise man. And he continued to abuse the disciple. But the more he insulted him, the more uproariously the seeker laughed. Finally, the wise man stopped and asked, "Why are you laughing?"

"For three years," said the seeker, "I had to pay the people who insulted me, and here you are giving it to me for free!"

The wise being looked into the eyes of the seeker and said, "Enter the city. It is all yours."

Kabir said, My Guru shows joy and sorrow to be one and the same. Once you realize this truth, you experience ecstasy, the ecstasy of union.

Reflecting the Light of the Supreme

The Lord says, "Among the heavenly bodies, I am the moon." The moon is so captivating. The full moon calls for you. The full moon makes you experience God's strength.

Why is the moon so important? Why does everyone like the moon so much? She is the moving lake of nectar in the sky. As she moves, she reflects the light of the sun. This is why she is so important. And this is why discipleship is much more important than Guruhood.

I remember during Baba's time when I was translating his talks, many people would say to me, "You know, I have to confess. When Baba was speaking, I would be watching you, and I wanted to become like you. I hope it's not wrong."

I would smile and say, "It's really better if you focus on the Guru's light. I'm just reflecting his light. He is the supreme light."

Now I hear that many people say to the wonderful students of Siddha Yoga meditation, "You know, more than Gurumayi, I watch you. I hope it's okay." Of course, the disciples say, "No. You should be watching Gurumayi. I'm just reflecting the light of the Guru."

We never stop being disciples. Just as the universe never stops reflecting the light of God, we never stop being disciples. We continue to reflect the light of the Supreme. This is the beauty of discipleship, and this is the beauty of the universe: it reflects the light of God. Everything reflects the light of God. So seeing God in everything should become a very easy and joyful practice.

Tell me, how long can you really look at the sun? But the moon—you can keep watching and watching her. Just keep watching her.

Early yesterday morning I went out to watch the moon set. When the moon is setting, her beauty is magnificent. So I went out to watch her change her attire. She has so many hats and so many robes. Each time she sets she wears different shades of color—and they never clash. She is perfect, this moon, this moving lake of nectar. I watched her for a long time until she sank behind the trees. She was marvelous. When I got up, I realized the ground I had been sitting on was very rough. But the softness of the moon, her perfection, her reflection, her way of being and her way of moving had entranced me. I was captivated by everything she conveyed, everything she lived for. It was amazing to sit on the hard ground and still experience the softness of the moonbeams.

This is why she is so special, and this is why we like the moon: she reflects the light of the sun. She reflects the light of the supreme Self, and therefore we worship her.

The poet asks, "What is there in thee, Moon, that thou should'st move my heart so potently?" Kabir says, "O sadhus, my heart delights in my Sadguru." Baba says, "The sacred water is inside you. It will cleanse you." And Jnaneshwar Maharaj calls her, "The moving lake of nectar in the sky."

The Full Moon Rising in Your Heart

Sit quietly now for a few moments. Breathe in deep, breathe out long. Allow the breath to become full. Allow the moving lake of nectar to spring forth within you. Your entire being is the inner space, the inner ether, the inner sky. Allow yourself to become submerged in the moving lake of nectar in the inner sky. Allow your heart to soak in the moving lake of nectar, the full moon. Let every cell of your body shine, let every cell be filled with ecstasy. Watch the full moon rising in your heart. Watch the full moon rising in the *sahasrāra*, the crown of the head. Ease into this moving lake of nectar. Allow yourself to become saturated in the moving lake of nectar in the inner sky. As you experience the fullness of the breath, experience the fullness of ecstasy.

And don't tell me you only got a dry chapati! Chew it! You will taste the nectar! Happy, happy, happy Guru Purnima.

With great respect, with great love, I welcome you all with all my heart.

Sadgurunāth mahārāj kī jay!

Guru Purnima

Chapter 2

The Light of the Guru's Feet

With great respect, with great love, I welcome you all with all my heart.

Happy Guru Purnima weekend. The moon is full and our hearts are also very full. We are surrounded within and without by the glory of the supreme Guru. It is wonderful to speak about the supreme Guru, who abides in our hearts, who makes our lives more meaningful.

At the opening of *Play of Consciousness*, Baba Muktananda offers salutations to his Guru, Bhagawan Nityananda, his supreme Lord, his supreme Shiva, in this way:

> I invoke the lotus feet of Nityananda, the supreme Guru,
> who is the blessing of all blessings, whose glance destroys
> all misfortunes and bestows supreme good fortune.

I invoke the Guru, who is *parabrahman*, the supreme Absolute, who is free from stain and completely pure, whose presence easily bestows the state of *parabrahman*.

The saints of India sing about the importance of the Guru; they explain why Guru's grace is so necessary in one's life. Although their songs appear to be in praise of the Guru, truly speaking, they depict what the disciples had to go through and what they finally attained. These songs also make you understand why the disciples worship the Guru.

In one of her songs, Mirabai, a great saint of India, says:

My mind is completely one with the Guru's feet.
I love my Guru's feet.
My mind is completely entangled in the Guru's feet.
There is nothing else in this world
I truly desire except my Guru's feet.
Everything else that I was so enmeshed in
in my life is false, is an illusion.
Everything else that I thought gave me life,
truly speaking, took away my life.
My mind is one with my Guru's feet.

Invoking the Power of Grace

The Guru's feet represent grace. They represent shakti. When we speak about the Guru's feet, we are not referring to the physical body of the Guru as such. We are invoking the benevolent power of grace that constantly flows through the compassionate form of the Guru.

Whenever you become aware of weak points in your life, all you have to do is remember the Guru's feet. Just as the moon gives us her liquid rays, in the same way, the Guru's feet give us divine light. This light takes away all difficulties. And therefore, Mirabai says, I love my Guru's feet. My mind is entangled in my Guru's feet.

Baba Muktananda taught us that the Guru's feet actually dwell in the crown chakra of the head, in the *sahasrāra*. If you keep your attention focused on the crown chakra where the Guru's feet abide, then the lotus of the heart chakra remains open. Just as the night-blooming lotus opens when the moon rises, in the same way, the heart lotus within you remains open as nectar flows down from the Guru's feet. When this happens, your vision becomes clear and discerning. You become stronger. This is when you truly experience your own courage.

Where Does Your Mind Take You?

The message for this year is "Wake up to your inner courage and become steeped in divine contentment." Many people have embraced this message fully, while others tell me how much they have struggled with it. Many people have made great progress by understanding the intricacies of this message and the subtleties of their own sadhana. Yet there are other people who use the message to run away from their responsibilities and duties. They say, "Well, I'm not courageous, so why should I even try to do that? I'm not content, so why should I accept this?"

The mind often makes excuses in this way. It takes something, whether beautiful or ordinary, and uses it to justify its own tendencies. If you do not witness how your mind plays tricks, then you are completely fooled by its antics. The amazing thing is that most people are not embarrassed about being tricked in this way; they are not ashamed of being controlled by their own mind. However, they are afraid that if you are on the spiritual path you will be controlled by someone else, that if you chant in a foreign language your brain will be programmed. But look at your own mind! What does your mind do to you day in and day out? Where does it take you?

When you are chanting in the meditation hall, your body is sitting in paradise; but where is your mind? Where are you really? Of course, when most of you chant, you are completely suffused with the energy of the chant, you are swimming in the extraordinary nectar of chanting. But then there must be times when your body is here, and your mind is . . . where *is* your mind?

Someone once told me of a saying: God wanted us to follow Him, not because He needed our help, but because He knew loving Him would make us whole. There is so much truth in these words. By loving God, who benefits? By loving the Guru, who benefits? By experiencing love in your own heart, who really benefits? As much as you may think you love God, truly speaking, God feels an even greater amount of love for you. And He is always waiting to give and give to you. He is always waiting to embrace you. No matter how much you think you love God, God gives you so much more love. And this has always been the case. If you really think about your own life, you love God a certain amount, yet you receive more than you can ever handle. So when Mirabai says, Let your mind be entangled in the Guru's feet, you don't have to be afraid that someone is going to take advantage of you or that the Guru's feet are going to take your mind away. This kind of love makes you whole.

Beyond All External Attire

Someone once asked Baba Muktananda, "Can you read people's minds?" Baba's reply was, "What makes you think I'm interested in playing with people's garbage?" Don't misunderstand this statement. Baba looked beyond the impurities of the mind and saw the divine light. In fact, once when someone asked him, "When you see a person, what do you really see?" Baba said, "The Blue Pearl. I see the Blue Pearl. Then everything else comes into focus, and I see the person's face and hands and feet and I hear what the person is saying."

This was demonstrated once very concretely when Baba

was giving darshan in the Oakland Ashram. Many, many seekers were coming for darshan, and Baba was brushing their heads with the peacock feathers, handing out mantra cards, giving spiritual names, having casual conversations, and sometimes holding deep philosophical discussions. It was like a river flowing before him, and he was acknowledging everyone exactly as they were. At one point someone came forward and, once again, Baba nodded and brushed his head with the feathers. As the person started to walk away from darshan, the entire hall cracked up. People were howling with laughter. Baba looked around because for him nothing unusual had taken place. He couldn't understand why people were laughing so hard. Then he asked, "Why is everyone laughing?"

I said, "Baba, look, look!" A clown had just come for darshan and was standing on the side waiting for Baba's attention.

"Where? Where?" asked Baba.

And I kept saying, "Over there, Baba. He's standing there. You see that hat and that attire and all the polka dots? You see?"

And then finally, Baba burst into his wonderful laughter. He laughed and pounded on his thighs, and brushed the people a little harder with the feathers. Then he announced to everyone, "Look, look, there's a clown! Look, a clown!" People were so happy that Baba had noticed the clown. I remember thinking about this incident all day long and for many weeks to come, and even to this day I contemplate it. Baba saw something within us that was so much more precious and so much more blissful than our external attire.

See the Shakti Shimmering

When you attach your mind to the shakti, to the grace of the Guru's feet, you become cleansed and charged with great power. You need this grace to do spiritual practices. There are so many times in your life, even on the most wonderful spiritual path, when you lose heart, you lose courage. You think contentment is out of your reach. That is why you need to remember that God loves you. You need to place your mind in the right place. You need to place your mind at the Guru's feet. When you truly meditate on the Guru's feet, you don't see toes and ankles and bones; you see shakti shimmering.

This is why in Siddha Yoga meditation, we believe in sharing our experiences as much as we believe in silence and solitude. When you share your beautiful experiences of chanting, of meditating, of doing seva, the subtle vibrations of these practices shimmer in the air. At such times, you don't see others as just flesh and bones, but as the shakti, as grace. Then, when you speak to someone from this pure place, you can truly make the right connection. Otherwise, a hard crust begins to form, and you can't even hear the voice of the Guru; you can't experience the light of your own heart.

For this reason, have the experience of being in the sacred heart, and then interact with your neighbor, knowing that in this place you are safe, you are secure. You don't have to worry that someone is going to take advantage of you. You don't have to imagine that your courage is going to seep away or your contentment is going to disappear. If you learn to visit this place again and again, then when you receive even a small morsel of *prasād*, you know you are living in paradise. You know you have attained everything.

The Ocean of Worldliness

Mirabai says, If you place your mind at the Guru's feet, you attain everything.

> I don't want anything anymore.
> My mind is entangled in the Guru's feet.

And this entanglement is not a punishment, it is beautiful. You can actually experience God's universe as it is.

> My mind is entangled in the Guru's feet.
> I worship the Guru's feet.
> Because I worship the Guru's feet,
> the ocean of worldliness has dried up completely.
> I am not afraid of going across anymore.

Such a great attainment! What is this ocean of worldliness? It's not something outside. It's not the Pacific Ocean or the Atlantic. The ocean of worldliness is the unbridled mind. The Guru's feet are so powerful that when the mind is attached to them, they dry up the ocean of worldliness in the mind. Even if you have negative thoughts, somehow the light from the Guru's feet turns these thoughts into a form of guidance. You think something is negative only to find out—no, there is a great meaning in it. At times you may have terrible feelings. If the mind is attached to the Guru's feet, then their light makes you realize the feelings are not really terrible. Actually, they are a good omen; they are telling you, "Don't go in this direction." They are saying, "You shouldn't be talking to that person in that way. You shouldn't be performing that action." What you think is a terrible feeling is not really taking you away from the truth: it is showing you something helpful. You can only understand this when your mind is purified by the Guru's feet.

As Mirabai says, If the mind is entangled in the Guru's feet, then you experience God's universe as it is; you know the significance of everything that is happening. The ocean of worldliness is completely dried up.

Again and again Mirabai sings, My mind is entangled in my Guru's feet. *Mohe lāgī lataka guru charanana kī. Lataka* is an interesting word in Hindi. It can mean "entangled" and it also carries many other meanings. One way of translating *lataka* is "hanging on to things." Isn't this so descriptive of what the mind does? It is always *lataka*-ing, always hanging on to things.

For example, haven't you noticed that your mind often hangs on to the not-so-great things that are said about you? If someone says, "You are great. You are wonderful. You are beautiful. You are smart. You are intelligent. You are a genius. You are so graceful," you may not pay too much attention. People may sing your praises like a *sahasranāma*, they may chant a thousand praises to your virtues, and you may scarcely notice. However, just let them say one small critical thing, "I didn't really like what you did." And that's it! You turn your back. "We're finished!" And you hang on to it, you don't let go. The mind is *lataka*-ing all the time.

This is why Mirabai uses that word *lataka*. Of course, her mind is hanging on to something much more sublime. She says, My mind is *lataka*-ing to the Guru's feet; my mind is hanging on to the Guru's feet. The Guru's feet represent light; they represent energy, beauty, glory, upliftment, compassion, gratitude, salvation, freedom, abundance, solace, courage, contentment.

Let the Inner Vision Be Real

Mirabai says:

> My mind is completely entangled in the Guru's feet.
> My Lord, Giridhara, is so sweet.
> He is always looking after me.
> Since I have focused my mind on the Guru's feet,

my attention has turned inward.
My gaze has turned inward.

Baba Muktananda said, "If you are constantly looking outward, then you always find flaws. When you turn your gaze inward, you see the supreme light. You are able to recognize goodness in others."

When you chant the name of God, your gaze actually turns within. This is why we spend so much time in chanting. Chanting is one of the greatest practices. There comes a point when your gaze appears to be outside, but your focus is inward. You are experiencing the inner nectar. And this is the purpose of all our spiritual practices: they take us inside. Inside there is everything. And then you begin to live from that space. All our celebrations, retreats, programs, Intensives, all our courses, our sevas, contemplations, satsangs—everything is for this one purpose of turning inward.

Mirabai says, My gaze has turned inward. Baba reminds us, Look within. There is a great treasure. So don't look at the Guru and constantly wonder, "Did the Guru notice me? Is she talking to me?" This will never suffice; you will never be satisfied. You will only find deficiencies in what is given to you. With this outlook, you are receiving only with your flesh and bones, and flesh and bones are temporary. They cannot really hold everything you are meant to receive, everything you deserve. Your mind can play tricks. Your mind can twist the Guru's words; it can distort the words of wisdom that it receives from fellow seekers. So you have to go beyond your usual perception and make the inner vision the real vision. Then when the mind plays tricks, you are able to see beyond the initial darkness.

When there is a solar eclipse and the sun is completely obscured, scientists call it "totality." They say there is great beauty behind the apparent darkness. The colors and the brightness are exquisite. It is such a beautiful sight that many scientists try to have the darshan of this totality.

If the mind is completely absorbed in the Guru's feet, then even if negativities arise and you feel the light of the mind has been eclipsed, you still are able to see the beauty beyond the darkness. The mind is not really in darkness. No matter what thoughts go through the mind, the gaze has turned inward, and the mind is able to see the true Self. And then, when you read the scriptures, you are able to understand why they speak so highly of the Guru's grace, the Guru's teachings.

Find Yourself at the Guru's Feet

Sit quietly for a few minutes now and allow your mind to find itself at the Guru's feet. You may experience the Guru's feet in the crown of the head or in the heart region. Remember, the heart lotus blooms vibrantly. When the nectar from the Guru's feet falls upon this lotus, each petal is illuminated. Your heart feels brighter. It soars, it sings. Allow your gaze to turn inward. Watch the mind. No matter how many thoughts arise, allow the mind to remain in the company of the Guru's feet. Abide in the heart. Receive the Guru's *prasād* from this seat. Perceive the world from this space. Rest in the awareness: my mind is absorbed in the light of the Guru's feet. Hold this experience within yourself. Keep your mind absorbed in the Guru's feet. It is this conviction that actually makes your heart remain open and allows you to drink the nectar of the Guru's feet.

Don't Think It Only Happens to Saints

When you contemplate how your mind can be absorbed in the Guru's feet, different images may arise. For instance, you may see your awareness as a ripe fruit hanging from a great tree, the glorious tree of God. Even though the fruit is ripe, it is still receiving so much from the tree, and in turn it is adding its own beauty. When your mind is hanging from this tree, there is no danger of its vanishing. It will remain in this relationship forever. But you must be careful not to let the six enemies— anger, greed, jealousy, pride, desire, and delusion—break off the little branch that keeps the ripe fruit attached to the tree.

In India, the mango is the king of fruits, so I like to think of the mango tree and the luscious ripe fruit hanging from its branches. There are so many other images you can come up with—for instance, the full moon hanging from the sky.

You can create your own personal images for *lataka* and record them in your journal. Discover whatever image will help you to remember this teaching of Mirabai: my mind is attached to my Guru's feet.

The Guru's feet can be anywhere: in the voice of a little child or the singing of a bird. They can be there when some-one asks you to do something you don't want to do, when you have to study for an exam, when you are asked to make an appearance and you don't want to show up. Whatever it is, stay open. You will find the Guru's feet. You can find them anywhere—not just in meditation, not just in your *pūjā* room, not just in the ashram, but in your office, on the highway, in the market, or the schoolroom. Have conviction. You will find them. This conviction keeps your heart open and allows you to drink the nectar of the Guru's feet.

So keep your mind totally absorbed in the Guru's feet. I know I have repeated this again and again. And I know you have gotten the message. But now I am talking to the part of you that may want to forget your experience of the Guru's protection. I am talking to the part of you that may try to deny your own greatness. I am talking to the part of you that forgets your love and faith in the Guru. I am talking to the part of you that puts yourself down and makes you feel dry.

When Mirabai says, "My mind is attached to the Guru's feet," don't think it only happens to saints. It can happen to you too. When you love the highest, only the highest things happen to you. You are able to see the highest in everything. Allow the love that has been awakened in your heart to remain at the Guru's feet. Then you won't ever get lost in the ocean of worldliness.

With great respect, with great love, I welcome you all with all my heart.

Sadgurunāth mahārāj kī jay!

Rakhi Day

Rakhi Day

Chapter 3

Wrapped in God's Protection

———⟋◯⟍———

With great respect, with great love, I welcome you all with all my heart.

Happy Rakhi Day. One minute before our program began this morning, the moon reached its fullness, and it will continue to be full until this evening. Allow the nectar of the full moon to permeate your heart.

In India, this particular full moon is called the Nariyal Purnima. *Nāriyal* means coconut, and this is the time when many people go to the ocean or to a river or a stream and offer coconuts to these beautiful aspects of nature. In this way, they are giving back to the Earth what they have received from her. In the Native American tradition, this month's full moon is known as the Moon of Ripening, the Red Plums Moon, the

Big Harvest, the Time of Freshness. How appropriate for this moment—the time of freshness.

Now the summer is moving toward its peak. This is a time when your fresh energy is very much needed, and you need to take good care of yourself. When the end of something is in sight, it is easy to become careless and lose everything—your enthusiasm, your support, your connection. Therefore, this is a critical time. You have to reassess all you have done. You must take the merits of your sadhana and utilize them.

When something is reaching its climax, it is important to experience the fullness of your own being. You have given so much just to reach this point, and now you can give more. You have given so much to your sadhana, and you can give more. It is important to complete whatever you are doing with great enthusiasm and courage, with even more wonderful contentment and splendid generosity.

At times like this, you may think, "I've given so much! Now it's everyone else's turn." This kind of thinking reveals the human plight, and it is very sad. Many people give, and then there comes a time when they think, "Why should I? I've given so much. Who cares about me? Does anyone think of me? Does God care about me? Does the Guru understand me? Will anyone be there when I am dying?" The mind likes to take a negative turn just at this point, when things are coming to a conclusion. If you find that your mind is doing this, look back and recall why you came to this path in the beginning.

It Takes Courage to Accept Change

Why does a person approach the Guru? Initially, you come to the Guru seeking the highest, wanting the Truth. The Guru gives you shaktipat and an explosion takes place. Your life is transformed; wonderful things are revealed. By "wonderful" I mean wonder-filled. Now wonder-filled experiences may be good or bad, depending on your attitude, your perception. Whatever they may be, they are filled with wonder. They take your breath away. You want to know what extraordinary thing is happening to you.

Somehow, after a while, you forget all this. You forget this gift from the Guru. Instead of experiencing the wonder of what you have already received, you begin to think, "Will the Guru give me a *rākhī* today? Is anyone going to notice me? Will the Guru speak to me? Will she talk nicely about me to other people? What will she give me?"

At such a moment, shaktipat is forgotten. The revelation of heaven is forgotten. Transformation is forgotten. All the cups of nectar that have been given to you are forgotten—out the window, gone—and the mind takes a negative turn. "Will Gurumayi walk my way? Will she send someone to give me a spiritual discourse?" The focus is on "What will I get? What will I get from the Guru? What will I get from the ashram? What will I get from Siddha Yoga meditation?"

It really doesn't matter how much you give to people; they have a tendency to forget. It is people's nature to forget what they have received from God, from the Guru, from this universe. Sometimes this tendency is spoken of as ignorance. In this state of ignorance, a stupor comes over you. You just doze off and you forget everything you have received. Gratitude has disappeared. There is only the desire for more and more — more from the Guru, more from God, more from the universe. Such a plight.

Often after people receive shaktipat, it is difficult for them to speak about how their life has been transformed, how they have changed. Have you ever wondered why this is? Baba said, "It takes courage to accept change as a gift from God." Instead of remembering the immense gift of grace they have received, instead of contemplating the changes in their life, the focus is on getting: "What will the ashram give me? What will I be given?" As long as you are able to forget all you have received, your bowl of desires will never be filled. It doesn't matter how much more you receive from the Guru, from this universe. It will just be a waste of your time and a waste of God's time.

Real Human Thinking

The other day someone was speaking to me about two schools of philosophical thought. One is associated with Vasishtha and the other with Vishvamitra, two sages of India who were greatly revered and honored. Vishvamitra gave his teachings to more and more people. He believed the more he gave, the better it was. As a result, he had thousands of disciples, many great-hearted but ordinary seekers who followed his teachings. Vasishtha had a different viewpoint. He chose his disciples carefully, so there were very few of them. However, Vasishtha was able to create giants, brilliant-minded people.

This is something to think about. Is it really good to give more and more? Or is it better to think about those few people who will receive the knowledge and understand it thoroughly, who will save it and savor it, and then hand it on to future generations?

Once there was an old, old man who was planting a very small mango tree. With great care, he was planting this tiny tree. A passerby asked the old man, "How long do you think it will take for this tree to grow and bear fruit?"

"It depends on nature," said the old man.

"Well, could you make a guess?"

"If nature is very good, it will take five to ten years for this tree to grow big enough to give fruit."

"Do you think you will be alive then to enjoy the fruit?"

The old man was puzzled and said, "What do you mean,

will I be alive? Of course! I will be alive in the people of future generations. I'm not planting this just for my sake. I want to do something for the next generation. I want them to enjoy the fruit from this tree."

This is called real human thinking. The other way—forgetting what you have received from God—is called bestial thinking. Of course, even beasts don't think only about themselves all the time. It usually happens only when they are hungry or afraid.

Real human thinking is preserving the shakti and always having the yearning to give. Even when you know your sadhana is not yet complete, and you know there is more to experience and more to understand, if you have the impulse to help people, to give of yourself, this is human thinking. This is how to be a true human being. As long as there is only taking, there is going to be suffering in this world.

Once in Gurudev Siddha Peeth during a Christmas retreat, some devotees had donated a fabulous Christmas tree with beautiful ornaments. The tree looked brilliant and people were delighted. In those days the management of the ashram had become a bit lax and the *gurukula* policy was not practiced as carefully as it is now. There were thousands and thousands of people at the celebration, and some of them were not really seekers.

One day after the Christmas celebrations were over, a small group of people, both adults and children, began to rip the Christmas tree apart. They had forgotten where they were and why they were there. They had forgotten all about the breathtaking retreat: the chanting and meditation; the great shakti and love shimmering in the air; the hours spent in Baba's Samadhi Shrine, Bade Baba's Temple, the meditation cave, and the gardens. These visitors forgot all this, and they were grabbing the ornaments from the tree. It was a scene to behold—the Christmas tree was being torn apart, ornament by ornament. As people were snatching things from the tree, they were shoving and pushing one another and the ornaments broke. They were beautiful and delicate; some of them were tiny. They needed to be handled with care, with love—not greed, not envy, not with the attitude "What will I get?" So these people were deprived of this *prasād*. Those ornaments weren't just ordinary ornaments; they carried the shakti of Gurudev Siddha Peeth, the shakti of the Siddhas. These people had forgotten the shakti they had received.

You Are on the Path of Liberation

As long as there is this tendency to forget what you receive, there will be suffering. As long as there is this attitude of "What will I get now? What will I get tomorrow? What will I get next week?" the suffering in this world will not come to an end. It will increase.

You may hold conferences to remove hunger or to bring about peace in the world. International organizations may put on one seminar after another, one conference after another, but as long as there is forgetfulness, as long as you have this attitude of "What will I get?" very little good will come from such activities. They may feed your ego. But take away suffering from the world? No, not unless there is true giving. Let us not be blind; let us be honest. Let us have the courage to face the truth.

Wake up to your inner courage and become steeped in divine contentment. Waking up to your inner courage does not mean putting on a brave face. You may be crying, you may be falling apart, but you can still be courageous. What gives you support is your inner conviction.

Everything on the outside can change. When you put wax in fire, it melts; it looks like the wax is crying. But you can take that melted wax and create something even more beautiful. People used to bring me wonderful big candles made from the leftover wax of the candles they burned at the Siddha Yoga meditation centers or at home. They would put their creative energy into the project, and then they would bring the candles in darshan. I was always so touched to see that these people didn't think melted wax was a waste. They saw the universe in it; they saw their own creative power manifesting.

Waking up to your inner courage doesn't mean putting on a brave face or making smart remarks or daring to sit with someone you don't like. That is not courage. Sometimes people say, "Well, I have courage now. I can go up to people and talk to them." Are those people wearing tiger and lion masks? Is that why you are so afraid? That is not what is meant by courage.

If you have received shaktipat, truly contemplate your experience. How has it changed your life? For better or worse, face it. Some people like to tell me, "Well, before I received shaktipat, everything was fine. After I received shaktipat, I had two accidents, I lost five jobs, and my family doesn't talk to me. And I don't know what to do, I'm full of depression." What you need to understand is that these things would have happened to you anyway. They didn't happen because you received shaktipat.

You know how it is when you cut your finger: you put hydrogen peroxide on it and it stings. Now you can't blame the stinging on the peroxide. You are the one who got the cut. The germs are on your hand, not in the peroxide. You can't blame what is helping you clean up the problem.

In India, there is a saying: If you bite the hand that feeds you, what hope is there for you? Sometimes when a mother is feeding her child, he may bite her hand. Of course, you can understand this—he's only a child. But you are a grown-up. You have received shaktipat. You have matured. You are on the path of liberation. You want to create heaven on earth. So if you forget the hand that is feeding you, what hope is there for you? That is not courage—to kill the very thing that is giving you life.

Why Can't You Be Happy?

In India, there is a sad situation. If someone is regarded as a holy person, then many people want to come for his darshan. They want to touch his feet, his knees, his elbows. They just try to grab him without any consideration for him as a person, without any consideration for the physical manifestation of the grace-bestowing power of God.

It is like what happened to India herself over and over again when other countries invaded her. India was very rich, and the invaders particularly looted temples because they were studded with jewels. To this day there are huge holes in the temples where there had been jewels. And people do the same kind of thing to anyone who is considered a holy person or a saint or a Guru—they go and try to grab. Why? Because they have not experienced the teachings, they haven't felt the truth of them within their own being.

Once you truly experience the deep silence that comes from a holy person, all you want to do is serve. You want to express your courage and live in contentment. Think about how, having received shaktipat from the Guru, your life has been transformed. Think about what you have been able to give to others. Talk about the positive things you have experienced. It will do a lot of good. Don't complain about the difficulties in your life. There is no reason to make other people's minds a garbage dump for your negativities. Form your own recycling company!

It's Rakhi Day. Last night the full moon was gorgeous, and today everyone has been beaming. I was told that the devotees in California and Mexico, who have joined us today by audio broadcast, have been chanting this morning with all their hearts. In fact, just before I began my talk, someone put a note on my side table with special news from the Santa Barbara center. I wanted to read the note to you, but when I looked for it just now, it was gone. If it had been bad news, it probably would have been left there! When it's bad news, people come running to the Guru; they don't waste a minute. In India, if people see a holy person, they think they should only talk about the problems in their lives. This used to happen to Baba all the time, and I wondered why people did that. The practice has continued into the next generation. People come to me and paint a picture of the doom in their lives. And of course, your heart bleeds when you hear their sad stories. But as soon as they go two steps away, they meet their friends and are hugging and kissing and laughing; they are talking nicely and feeling wonderful. When they come before the Guru, they have a very sad story. Then you see them in the dining room, in the gardens, in the courses, or taking a walk, and they are happy. Only in front of the Guru do they have sad faces. People like to bring the Guru bad news, but if it's good news they think, "Oh, the Guru is in such a high state. Why does she need to hear good news anyway? Good news is for other people who need it."

I want you to know I am very much aware of all the good things that have been given to you, all the beautiful things Baba has given you, all the care you have received in the centers and ashrams. I am very much aware of all the hard work that people do—the swamis, the brahmin priests, the directors, the scholars, the teenagers, the children, the older people, and all the sevites. I know thousands and thousands of people all over the world who work extremely hard. They give their time and money and energy, they give their strength and well-being to help bring happiness to your life. So why can't you be happy? Why can't you revel in the great things that are happening?

What if there are a few difficulties? The show must go on. Your life must continue with dignity, with splendor and honor, with great generosity.

Someone just handed me the missing note. It says that the Santa Barbara center called to let us know it is raining there. They have had no rain for many, many months, and there were several big forest fires burning. As soon as we all started chanting this morning in our various locations—here and in Mexico and in California—it began to rain in Santa Barbara. Chanting has so much power. You might think of chanting as an ordinary practice, but truly speaking, with so many people throughout the world chanting, creating a wonderful atmosphere through their voices, an incredible power is created. Never underestimate the power of pure chanting.

Share Your Good News with Others

It truly is okay to share good news. It helps to glorify God. By sharing the good news about your transformations since shaktipat, it's not that you are glorifying the Guru or the greatness of Siddha Yoga meditation, or that you are trying to bring more people to this organization. No. You don't want just more people. Do you know what they say in museums? They say that the more people who come, the sooner the precious items in the museum deteriorate. There is something about the heat and energy from so many people that is harmful to the objects in the museum. It's not that you want just more and more people. You want to bring true seekers, people who have been touched by your experiences, who are willing to give their lives for the betterment of humanity, who are yearning to see God face-to-face. The energy coming from such people is invigorating, it is enlivening.

In fact, Baba used to say, "If someone has received shaktipat, then meditate next to that person. *You* will receive shaktipat as well." Many times when people complained to Baba that their husband or their wife or their child didn't want to come to Siddha Yoga meditation programs, Baba would say, "Don't worry. Sometime just quietly sit next to them and meditate. You can go into meditation, and they will receive the shakti." And that is the truth.

The energy that comes from those who have received shaktipat, whose lives have been transformed, is precious, it is beneficial. That energy will actually preserve the shakti and make it grow. It is like the *yajña* fire. You want to sit before the *yajña* fire because it has been charged with mantras by the brahmin priests and by your good wishes. That fire is good. It is energizing, vivifying. It gives you life.

So share your good news with others. When it's bad news, learn how to contemplate what is happening. Learn how to process things within yourself, and then give the best to the world. If you fall down while you're walking along the road, don't make a big fuss. But if you find a precious stone, tell everyone about it. In fact, give it away to someone.

The Fire of the Awakened Shakti

Today is Rakhi Day and it is known as the day of protection. Although protection is always present, we have to learn how to wrap ourselves in God's protection. Baba Muktananda concludes his book *Play of Consciousness* with a beautiful blessing about the protection of the Siddhas.

My dear, my own Siddha students! . . . Having been worthy of receiving the grace of a Siddha, you now belong to the Siddha lineage, your world is Siddhaloka. Your state is the same as that attained by the Siddhas. The most divine power of grace of countless great beings living in Siddhaloka stands behind you to protect you. May you be fully protected by this power of grace. This is my blessing.

Siddha students! Only a few sparks of fire can burn an entire forest to ashes. Similarly, even the tiny ray of the Siddhas' *chiti shakti* that has entered you burns away your impurities. May it grant you perfect Siddhahood. This is my blessing.

You are all rays of Siddha beings. You are all taking part in the play of *chiti shakti*. She is active within you. May you become saturated with Consciousness in the world you live in. . . . This is my blessing.

My supreme Guru, Shri Nityananda, is also my supreme deity. . . . May Lord Shri Guru Nityananda, whom I worship constantly, the inner Self of all, the activator of shakti and the chakras, enter into all my Siddha students, residing within them as their inner Self. May you fill their lives with bliss, O Bhagawan Nityananda. This is my blessing.

Sit quietly now for a few minutes. Understand that the precious breath you breathe in and out is charged with the Guru's shakti. Without ever judging you as high or low, great or small, good or bad, without ever looking at your impurities, the Guru's shakti simply enters you. The fire of the Guru's shakti burns away all impurities. Without judging you, the Guru's grace descends upon you. Your entire being is permeated with the Guru's grace.

Shaktipat is Baba Muktananda's divine mission. When the shakti is awakened within you, it gives you everything. By awakening your inner shakti, the Guru feeds you and clothes you, the Guru caresses you, the Guru holds you in his heart and makes you his own. By awakening the shakti within, he completely purifies you. The shakti is a treasure-house. By unlocking your heart, the Guru reveals your own divinity. This divinity contains great promise, both mundane and spiritual. When the shakti is awakened, you, who are a *nara*, a human being, become Narayana, the Lord.

Baba's light blazes inside your being. Allow your mind to revel in the deep silence of the heart. In the beginning you may find your heart is sad, your heart is full of conflicts. Stay with it. Keep going deeper. Let the tears roll down your cheeks. Let your entire being melt in the fire of shakti. Keep going deeper. You will find a beautiful space of silence. Although this space has total stillness, it is highly charged with shakti. Allow your mind to take repose in the deep silence of your being. When you allow yourself to go deeper into this silence, a great wonder, an incredible phenomenon, will take place. After you submerge yourself in this profound silence of your being, you will emerge with great liveliness, full of life, full of joy. You will emerge from this profound silence with tremendous shakti, a new perception, a true life.

The precious breath that you breathe in is charged with the mantra and the Guru's benevolent *sankalpa*. The breath that you breathe out is charged with the mantra and Baba's benevolent blessing. Contemplate this knowledge.

If You Have a Good Mind, You Can Do Almost Anything

When you receive the Guru's grace, the Guru's shakti, you receive protection. You don't have to try to protect yourself from this universe or from God or from the Guru. You have to protect yourself from the workings of your own mind. That is where you need protection. You never know when your mind may turn nectar into dirty water. That is why the Vedas say: "O my mind, always resolve on that which is noble, benevolent, and good." Again and again, bring your mind back to the source of happiness, to God, to the great things people do for you in your life.

Once a doctor shared with me that each time a particular devotee came for a treatment, he would say, "My body may be falling apart, but with Baba's grace my mind is always good." I was touched by that story. It is so important to have a good mind.

You don't really need protection from the elements or other people or animals or losing a job or not having enough money. It's your mind that needs protection. If you have a good mind, you can do almost anything. When you receive the Guru's grace and shakti, you are protected. You are saved from the afflictions of your own mind. Then you can put your mind to great use. Little children have good minds, and each of you was born with such a mind. It's just that as you grow up, something else happens.

So Much Wisdom Flowering in You

This morning I was tying a *rākhī* bracelet onto the wrist of a six-year-old boy. Even though he is only six years old, his vocabulary is quite big. He uses words like "impression" and "recognize." As I was tying the thread on his wrist and making a knot, it became too tight and I almost shuddered. I immediately tried to remove the knot and said, "I'm so sorry, I'm so sorry. Let me redo it."

He had such a bright smile on his face as he said, "Gurumayi, you are my Guru. You don't have the strength to hurt me. You only have the power to cuddle me."

What great understanding. I wish we could all have that understanding about Baba, about God, about this universe. Whenever something difficult happens, I wish we could all know that God doesn't have the strength to hurt us. God only has the power to give us love, to cuddle us, to always have us in His arms. Little children have this understanding, and I want to ask the parents to allow this wisdom in their children to grow.

The other day, a mother was complaining to me that her little boy behaves quite badly and is often out of control. She just doesn't know how to handle him. Even though he is only three years old, he has so much energy and a hot temper. I said, "Whatever you do, don't beat him. And don't yell at him. Speak to him like an adult. Don't speak to him like a little baby. When he is misbehaving, find the right time and talk to him. If you talk to him like an adult, his vocabulary will grow and he will be able to understand. If you beat him and yell at him, you are going to kill his spirit. Everyone needs that spirit to become a beautiful human being."

I learn so much from children. I like to be around them. Next summer we are going to focus on children and young people. The programs will be designed so I can spend more time with young people. You adults have already received so much. It is your time to impart the teachings to others. Don't keep begging; your begging bowl is overflowing. Share your wisdom with others. You can talk to people about your meditation, you can encourage and support them. You have gone to school and you know how to study. You can read Siddha Yoga meditation publications, yogic books, and the scriptures. You can also write. If you keep a journal of your experiences, you will find after a few years that not only have you come a long way in your sadhana, but your wishes have been fulfilled. If you don't keep a record of it, you will never know how much you have received from the Guru's grace. There is so much wisdom flowering in you. Don't let it wither with the workings of your mind.

Let It Blaze

It is really a happy Rakhi Day. It is the day of protection, the full moon. Allow the nectar of the full moon to permeate your entire being. Let the luster of the full moon shine forth. As you greet people, think of the full moon. When you see each person, think of the full moon shining in his or her face, and see what that does to your heart. Think of the full moon in an object or a word. If someone says, "*Om Namah Shivāya*," think of the full moon. If someone asks you to come and have ice cream, think of the full moon. No matter what the words are, think of the full moon and what it can do. You are all very full, so impart your wisdom to others.

Please do understand that Baba's blessings are with you. You can read Baba's benediction in *Play of Consciousness* again and again and realize how much he loves you. He loved people with unique characteristics, and he loved the most resistant people. So if you think you are one of those people who doesn't like to meditate, who doesn't like spiritual practices, if you think you are "a hellish worm" or "the lowest of the low," as Baba used to say, know that he loves you. He really loves you. He will come to you; he will hold your arm and shake you gently. He will pinch your cheek. He will look directly into your eyes, and he will say, "Good man, good man," or "Good woman, good woman." I remember seeing him do that over and over again.

Read Baba's benediction in *Play of Consciousness*. Your heart will be touched by his love. Baba truly loves everyone. Each time you remember how much he loves you, all you want to do is cry with gratitude for so much love. As a great saint sang:

> O great fire, O my Guru, just give me one spark.
> I don't ask for anything.
> I just want one touch, just one spark.

Baba has given each one of you not just a spark, but a great fire. He has kindled a great fire inside you. Let it blaze.

With great respect, with great love, I welcome you all with all my heart.

Sadgurunāth mahārāj kī jay!

New Moon
in September

New Moon in September

Chapter 4

Be at Ease, Be Thoughtful, Be Courageous, and Be Content

———⌒———

With great respect, with great love, I welcome you all with all my heart.

Today is a great day in the history of Siddha Yoga meditation. It is the lunar anniversary of Baba Muktananda's Divya Diksha day, the fiftieth anniversary of the day he received shaktipat from his Guru, Bhagawan Nityananda. Today is also the new moon day. In India, when the new moon falls on Monday, it is particularly special. Monday is Lord Shiva's day and the new moon is Lord Shiva's moon, so it is a sacred day. This also happens to be Labor Day, the North American holiday that traditionally marks the end of summer. We have reached the culmination of our summer retreat and the beginning of a new chapter in our lives.

In Siddha Yoga meditation, we love to celebrate. We celebrate solar anniversaries and lunar anniversaries; we love to celebrate every anniversary and each moment. It is truly magical to realize that today, once again, we have a chance to offer our gratitude to Baba Muktananda and to Bhagawan Nityananda. They have given us this life that contains great understanding, incredible changes, and magnificent challenges. Through their benevolent grace we have been awakened to a fantastic viewpoint—always knowing that everything happens for the best. Whether it's a sad moment or a happy moment, everything is blessed.

You Yourself Are Blessed

People used to come up to Baba Muktananda and say, "Baba, would you bless this necklace? I just bought it. Will you please bless it?"

And Baba would say, "Have you taken an Intensive? Have you received shaktipat?"

"Yes, Baba, I have."

"Well, *you* are blessed. Everything you touch is blessed. Why should I only bless the necklace? You yourself are blessed."

What great understanding we receive from such beings. Once you are touched by the shakti, you are truly blessed. You live in wisdom. You are enveloped by great love.

Death Gives Life to Life

I am certain there are many special occasions being celebrated today, many birthdays and anniversaries. But there are also many people who are shedding tears for the death of someone they loved. There is something about death. No matter how it happens—whether you die in a car accident or because of an illness, whether you die before you even come out of your mother's womb into this world—there is something about death. It touches the very core of your being. It doesn't matter whether it's your friend who dies or your enemy. In death, we are all equal. When it comes to death, no one is really special, no one is ordinary.

Somehow death teaches equality-consciousness. When you are alive in this world, you may work for many political causes; you may struggle long and hard for equality, for independence. Yet very few beings truly achieve the inner state of equal vision. Nonetheless, when death comes, it teaches everyone equality-consciousness. On the spot. Immediately. There is no hesitation.

Death makes life real. Death makes God true. Death brings death to all fights, to all illusions. It is very interesting how death exists in this world. Death is called a void. Death is supposed to take everything away, to put an end to everything. Yet it is death that gives life to life. Death gives life to God. Death gives life to your heart. Your heart may experience numbness throughout your life, but when death comes, your heart shudders. It stirs. There is Consciousness. You cry, you laugh. You feel something so true you cannot deny it. It makes your heart come alive. So powerful is death.

Death makes you question everything in a real way. In life, you question things, but then you forget. Death challenges you; it doesn't allow you to forget. Death makes you remember. It makes you continue your search. What a wonderful phenomenon death truly is.

The saints of India have always said there are only two things worth remembering in this world—God and death. No matter how you die, death says, "Wake up. O my dear one, wake up." Death makes you look at your own life: why you live, how you live, and more than anything else, what you are living for. If you know what you are living for, then you are truly living. If you have no idea what you are living for in this world, then your life can't even be called a living death—because in death there is awakening. In death, there is magic. In death, the heart comes alive. I am not talking about suicide—that kind of death has its own ugliness. I am talking about death that occurs on its own. In this death, there is beauty. In this death, something great happens.

Sometimes when the death is sudden and unexpected, people wonder what happens to the soul. When someone dies for whom people offer heartfelt prayers, there is no reason to be concerned about the soul. The prayers of loving hearts uplift that soul, along with many other souls suspended in the air and wanting the love of a human heart.

The love flowing from a human heart is nectarean, it is life-giving. The Indian scriptures say God takes birth on this planet to experience this love. Even God leaves His angels, His gods and goddesses, His heaven, to come and live with human beings on this planet. The love flowing from a human heart is truly life-giving. That love is worth more than anything else in this entire universe. Just for one drop of love flowing from a human heart, God takes birth. Just for one drop of such love, avatars live on this planet.

Don't Wait for Death to Teach You a Lesson

We have been exploring the message "Wake up to your inner courage and become steeped in divine contentment." Both courage and contentment appear in so many different forms. As a true seeker, it is right that you go into your heart again and again, that you be real with yourself and with others, that you be real with your Guru and with your responsibilities. You may hide everything during your life, but death will disclose it all to you. You will no longer be able to run away from whatever you are afraid of. Therefore the yogis of India say, "Don't wait for death to teach you a lesson." Learn all your lessons while you are still alive, while you can still see, hear, smell, speak, and touch. Imbibe each lesson with great reverence and gratitude.

I know there are some people who behave one way in front of the Guru and another way when they are somewhere else. They want the Guru to know certain things about them, and other things they don't want the Guru to know. But I want you to know that this kind of partial knowing will lead us nowhere. There is *another* kind of knowing, however. There is something that you and I both know, which can never be hidden. When you are in touch with your heart and I am in touch with my heart, we are completely connected. When you are in your heart and I am in my heart, we are actually in God's heart. In that heart, we know everything that we must know. In that union, in that love, we are together.

As the yogis of India say, "Learn everything in this universe with reverence and gratitude." Life continues to teach us many wondrous lessons, and they are always the ones we need to know at each particular moment. Embrace these lessons.

Life Will Enhance What You Offer It

During a *yajña*, a fire ritual, offerings are made to the fire. When you make an offering to the *yajña*, your face should be benevolent and happy, and your heart should also be benevolent and happy. You should make your offering with your virtues shining forth. Then that is what the fire will enhance; that is what the fire will radiate, will reflect back to you. If you frown when you are making your offering, a frowning face and attitude will be reflected back to you. If you turn your face away from the heat, that is the kind of attitude you will experience in your life. The spirit in which you make the offering is very important. The ingredients alone are not enough. It is the heart offering the ingredients that makes the difference.

In the same way, when challenges come in your life, accept them with a benevolent heart and face, with a happy heart and face. Accept the challenges with all your virtues shining forth, because those challenges will enhance what you offer to them. Life will enhance what you offer to life. Death will enhance what you give to death.

Therefore, understand: you must be real with your own heart. In that way, it will be easy for you to be real with others, and most of all, to be real with your own Guru, with your own inner Self. Why must you hide what your heart truly knows?

One Teaching in Your Heart

Sit quietly now for a few minutes. Allow yourself to imbibe what you have heard and felt. Learn to put your mind and heart at ease. Learn to put your entire body at ease, as the tireless breath comes in and goes out, comes in and goes out.

You have heard so many teachings. You have been surrounded by one great teaching after another. Take a moment now and choose one teaching that you want to imbibe fully. Place this teaching in your heart and contemplate it. Your mind is at ease. Your heart is at ease. Your whole body is at ease. Contemplate this one teaching that will save your life.

It is so powerful when you truly contemplate a teaching that you can accept, that your heart is able to embrace. It is so powerful when you make a resolution to follow a teaching, to really put it into practice and make it your own.

After you have contemplated this teaching, think about what has come up for you and then share it with others. You can speak to your friends, you can write a letter, you can write in your journal, and you can ruminate about this experience. Allow this contemplation to go on and on in your being, and you will see how it opens new dimensions for you. It will open new doors. It will give you a golden life. It will make you become aware of what a great life you already have.

As I practiced this contemplation, a beautiful *abhanga* by a great saint began to resound over and over in my mind. It is about the Guru's feet, the refuge for all.

> O Lord, whatever happens to this body,
> whether it remains alive or falls away,
> there is one thing I will never give up,
> and that is, forever and ever
> I will hold on to Your lotus feet.
> I will never give up Your lotus feet.
> I will always hold on to Your lotus feet.

For each one of you, there is a teaching that has come alive. Hold on to it. Later, you can share it with others.

Create a Glorious Destiny

Often after a program, people come to me and say, "Do you have a message for me? A special message?" Even though I have been speaking for one or two hours, they still ask for a message! Don't discard what you are given; learn to cherish every moment. Listen to everything with rapt attention. If you don't get good meditation one day, don't throw away all the great experiences you've had at other times. If someone isn't nice to you one time, don't forget all the thousands of people who have been kind and sweet and loving to you, who have given you everything. Just because you miss the bus, don't curse it. Think of the thousands of times when the bus came on time and you got a great seat.

Be at ease. Be thoughtful. You may be holding a beautiful crystal glass brimful with a wonderful beverage. Someone comes and makes you angry. Don't drop the crystal glass. Don't throw it at his head. Put it down and have a talk, have a dialogue. Be thoughtful. Just because one day you don't get the kind of food you want, don't become ungrateful. Think of all the times you've gotten so many wonderful dishes. Just because one time, just because one day, just because this person, just because this incident, just because, just because . . .

Rather than thinking in this way, gather all the great moments, all the wonderful moments. As you do this, you create a glorious destiny. Let it happen!

Be at ease. Be thoughtful. Be courageous and be content. Whatever happens, remember: The power of the Siddhas is with you. The grace of the Siddhas is with you. The love of the Siddhas is with you. Their protection is with you always.

With great respect, with great love, I welcome you all with all my heart.

Sadgurunāth mahārāj kī jay!

Sources

p. 7, Swami Kripananda, *Jnaneshwar's Gita* (Albany, N.Y.: SUNY Press, 1989). 15.371-73

p. 9, Alain Danielou, *The Gods of India: Hindu Polytheism* (New York: Inner Traditions International Ltd., 1985).

pp. 9-10, Daniel Ladinsky, *I Heard God Laughing: Renderings of Hafiz* (Walnut Creek, Calif.: Sufism Reoriented, 1996). Reprinted by permission.

Guide to Sanskrit Pronunciation

For the reader's convenience, the Sanskrit and Hindi terms most frequently used in Siddha Yoga meditation literature and courses appear throughout the text in roman type with simple transliteration. *Śaktipāta*, for instance, is shaktipat; *sādhanā* is sadhana, and so on. For less frequently used Sanskrit words, the long vowels are marked in the text. The glossary entries include the standard international transliteration for each Sanskrit term.

For readers not familiar with Sanskrit, the following is a guide for pronunciation.

Vowels

Sanskrit vowels are categorized as either long or short. In English transliteration, the long vowels are marked with a bar above the letter and are pronounced twice as long as the short vowels. The vowels e, ai, au, and o are always pronounced as long vowels.

Short:	Long:	
a as in c*u*p	*ā* as in c*a*lm	*ai* as in *ai*sle
i as in g*i*ve	*e* as in s*a*ve	*au* as in c*ow*
u as in f*u*ll	*ī* as in s*ee*n	*ū* as in sch*oo*l
ṛ as in w*ri*tten	*o* as in kn*ow*	

Consonants

The main differences between Sanskrit and English pronunciation of consonants are in the aspirated and retroflexive letters.

The aspirated letters have a definite *h* sound. The Sanskrit letter *kh* is pronounced as in ink*h*orn; the *th* as in boat*h*ouse; the *ph* as in loop*h*ole.

The retroflexes are pronounced with the tip of the tongue touching the hard palate; *ṭ*, for instance, is pronounced as in ant; *ḍ* as in end.

The sibilants are *ś*, *ṣ*, and *s*. The *ś* is pronounced as *sh* but with the tongue touching the soft palate; the *ṣ* as *sh* with the tongue touching the hard palate; the *s* as in history.

Other distinctive consonants are these:

c as in *ch*urch	*ṁ* is a strong nasal
ch as in pit*ch*-*h*ook	*ḥ* is a strong aspiration
ñ as in ca*ny*on	

For a detailed pronunciation guide, see *The Nectar of Chanting*, published by SYDA Foundation.

Glossary

ABHANGA [*abhaṅga*]
A devotional song in the Marathi language, expressing the longing and love of a devotee for God.

ABSOLUTE
The highest Reality; supreme Consciousness; the pure, untainted, changeless Truth.

ARJUNA [*arjuna*]
One of the heroes of the Indian epic *Mahābhārata*, considered to be the greatest warrior of all. He was the friend and devotee of Lord Krishna, who revealed the teachings of the *Bhagavad Gītā* to him on the battlefield. *See also* BHAGAVAD GITA; KRISHNA.

ASHRAM [*āśrama*]
The dwelling place of a Guru or saint; a monastic retreat site where seekers engage in spiritual practices and study the sacred teachings of yoga.

BABA MUKTANANDA.
See MUKTANANDA, SWAMI.

BADE BABA. *See* NITYANANDA, BHAGAWAN.

BHAGAVAD GITA [*bhagavadgītā*]
(*lit.*, song of God) One of the world's spiritual treasures and an essential scripture of Hinduism; a portion of the *Mahābhārata* in which Lord Krishna instructs his disciple Arjuna on the nature of the universe, God, and the supreme Self. *See also* ARJUNA; KRISHNA.

BHAGAWAN NITYANANDA.
See NITYANANDA, BHAGAWAN.

BLUE PEARL
A brilliant blue light, the size of a tiny

seed; the subtle abode of the inner Self, and the vehicle by means of which the soul travels from one world to another, either in meditation or at the time of death.

BRAHMIN [*brahmin*]

A caste of Hindu society whose members are by tradition priests and scholars.

CHAKRA [*cakra*]

(*lit.*, wheel) A center of energy located in the subtle body, where the subtle nerve channels converge like the spokes of a wheel. When awakened, the *kundalinī shakti* flows upward from the *mūlādhāra chakra* at the base of the spine to the seventh chakra, the *sahasrāra*, at the crown of the head. *See also* KUNDALINI; SAHASRARA; SHAKTIPAT.

CHITI SHAKTI [*citiśakti*]

The power of universal Consciousness; the creative aspect of God.

CONSCIOUSNESS

The intelligent, supremely independent, divine Energy, which creates, pervades, and supports the entire universe. *See also* ABSOLUTE; CHITI SHAKTI.

DARSHAN [*darśana*]

(*lit.*, to have sight of; viewing) A glimpse or vision of a saint; being in the presence of a holy person; seeing God or an image of God.

DIVYA DIKSHA [*divya dīkṣā*]

The bestowal of divine initiation, shaktipat.

GURU [*guru*]

A spiritual Master who has attained oneness with God and who is therefore able both to initiate seekers and to guide them on the spiritual path to liberation. A Guru is also required to be learned in the scriptures and must belong to a lineage of Masters. *See also* SHAKTIPAT; SIDDHA.

GURUDEV [*gurudeva*]

A respectful term of address, signifying the Guru as an embodiment of God.

GURUDEV SIDDHA PEETH

(*lit.*, abode of the perfected beings) The mother ashram of Siddha Yoga meditation, located in Ganeshpuri, India; the site of the Samadhi Shrine of Swami Muktananda. *See also* ASHRAM; SAMADHI SHRINE.

GURUKULA [*gurukula*]

(*lit.*, family or group of the Master) In Vedic times, spiritual aspirants would serve the Guru at his house or ashram for a period of time, studying the scriptures and practicing spiritual disciplines under the guidance of the Master. Siddha Yoga meditation ashrams are modeled on these *gurukulas* of old.

GURU PURNIMA [*gurupūrṇimā*]

(*lit.*, the full moon of the Guru) In India, the full moon of the month of Ashada (July-August) is honored as the most auspicious and important of the entire year. This moon's luminous brilliance and perfect form are seen as expressions of the Guru's gift of grace and the attainment of Self-realization.

GURU'S FEET

The Indian scriptures revere the Guru's feet, which are said to embody Shiva and Shakti, knowledge and action, the emission and reabsorption of creation. Powerful vibrations of shakti flow from the Guru's feet. They are a mystical source of grace and illumination, and a figurative term for the Guru's teachings.

HAFIZ
(1326-1390) A Sufi from Persia who was a court poet and professor. His ecstatic verse has delighted seekers for over six hundred years.

INTENSIVE
The primary Siddha Yoga meditation program, which was designed by Swami Muktananda to give spiritual initiation by awakening the *kundalinī* energy. *See also* KUNDALINI; SHAKTIPAT.

JNANESHWAR MAHARAJ
(1275-1296) Foremost among the poet-saints of Maharashtra, India; his best known work is *Jñāneshvarī*, a commentary in Marathi verse on the *Bhagavad Gītā*. At the age of twenty-one, Jnaneshwar took live *samādhi* (a yogi's voluntary departure from the body) in Alandi, where his samadhi shrine attracts thousands of seekers to this day.

KABIR
(1440-1518) A great poet-saint and mystic who lived as a simple weaver in Benares. His poems describe the universality of the Self, the greatness of the Guru, and the nature of true spirituality.

KASHMIR SHAIVISM
A branch of the Shaivite philosophical tradition, propounded by Kashmiri sages, that explains how the formless supreme Principle, known as Shiva, manifests as the universe. Together with Vedanta, Kashmir Shaivism provides the basic scriptural context for Siddha Yoga meditation.

KRISHNA [*kṛṣṇa*]
(*lit.*, the dark one) The eighth incarnation of Lord Vishnu. The spiritual teachings of Lord Krishna, called "the dark one" because of his deep blue skin, are contained in the *Bhagavad Gītā*, a portion of the epic *Mahābhārata*.

KUNDALINI [*kuṇḍalinī*]
(*lit.*, coiled one) The supreme power, the primordial energy (shakti) that lies coiled at the base of the spine. Through the descent of grace (shaktipat) this extremely subtle force is awakened and begins to purify the entire being. As *kundalinī* travels upward through the central channel, She pierces the various chakras, finally reaching the *sahasrāra* at the crown of the head. There, the individual self merges into the supreme Self, and the cycle of birth and death comes to an end. *See also* CHAKRA; INTENSIVE; SHAKTIPAT.

MAHASAMADHI [*mahāsamādhi*]
(*lit.*, the great union) 1) A realized yogi's conscious departure from the physical body at death. 2) A celebration on the anniversary of a great being's departure from the physical body. 3) A shrine erected at the place where a yogi has taken *mahāsamādhi*.

MANTRA [*mantra*]
(*lit.*, sacred invocation) The names of God; sacred words or divine sounds invested with the power to protect, purify, and transform the individual who repeats them. *See also* OM NAMAH SHIVAYA.

MIRABAI
(1433-1468) A Rajasthani queen famous for her poems of devotion to Lord Krishna. She was so absorbed in

love for Krishna that when she was given poison by vindictive relatives, Mirabai drank it as nectar and remained unharmed.

MUKTANANDA, SWAMI
(1908-1982) A Siddha of the modern age; Gurumayi Chidvilasananda's Guru, often referred to as Baba. This great yogi brought the powerful and rare initiation known as shaktipat to the West at the command of his own Guru, Bhagawan Nityananda.

NITYANANDA, BHAGAWAN
(d. 1961) A great Siddha Master, Swami Muktananda's Guru, also known as Bade Baba ("elder" Baba). He was a born Siddha, living his entire life in the highest state of consciousness. In both Gurudev Siddha Peeth in Ganeshpuri, India, and Shree Muktananda Ashram in South Fallsburg, New York, Swami Muktananda has dedicated a temple of meditation to honor Bhagawan Nityananda.

OM NAMAH SHIVAYA
[*oṃ namaḥ śivāya*]
(*lit.*, Om, salutations to Shiva) The Sanskrit mantra of the Siddha Yoga lineage; known as the great redeeming mantra because of its power to grant both worldly fulfillment and spiritual realization. *Om* is the primordial sound; *Namah* is to honor or bow to; *Shivāya* denotes divine Consciousness, the Lord who dwells in every heart.

PARABRAHMAN [*parabrahman*]
The supreme Absolute, whose nature is described in Vedantic philosophy as Existence, Consciousness, and Bliss.

PRANAM [*praṇāma*]
To bow; to greet with respect.

PRASAD [*prasāda*]
A blessed or divine gift.

PUJA [*pūjā*]
1) The performance of worship. 2) An altar with images of the Guru or deity and objects used in worship.

RAKHI DAY [*rākhī*]
This festival has its origins in an ancient folk custom: sisters affectionately tie a *rākhī*, or bracelet, on the wrists of their brothers who, in turn, promise always to protect them. To celebrate this day, many Siddha Yoga meditation students offer each other *rākhīs*, representing a bond of love and protection.

SADGURU [*sadguru*]
A true Guru; divine Master. *See also* GURU.

SADGURUNATH MAHARAJ KI JAY!
A Hindi phrase that means "I hail the Master who has revealed the Truth to me!" An exalted, joyful expression of gratitude to the Guru for all that has been received, often repeated at the beginning or end of an action.

SADHANA [*sādhanā*]
1) A spiritual discipline or path. 2) Practices, both physical and mental, on the spiritual path.

SADHU [*sādhu*]
A wandering monk or ascetic; a holy being; a practitioner of sadhana.

SAHASRANAMA [*sahasranāma*]
(*lit.*, one thousand names) A chant praising God in one thousand names. The *Vishnu Sahasranāma*, in which the many names of Lord Vishnu are sung,

is often chanted in Siddha Yoga meditation ashrams.

SAHASRARA [*sahasrāra*]

The thousand-petaled spiritual energy center at the crown of the head, where one experiences the highest states of consciousness. *See also* CHAKRA; KUNDALINI.

SAMADHI [*samādhi*]

The state of meditative union with the Absolute.

SAMADHI SHRINE

The final resting place of a great yogi's body. Such shrines are places of worship, permeated with the saint's spiritual power.

SANKALPA [*sankalpa*]

Thought or will directed toward a specific outcome. One of the four classical methods by which the Guru gives shaktipat.

SATSANG [*satsanga*]

(*lit.*, the company of the Truth) The company of saints and devotees; a gathering of seekers for the purpose of chanting, meditation, and listening to scriptural teachings or readings.

SELF

Divine Consciousness residing in the individual, described as the witness of the mind or the pure I-awareness.

SEVA [*sevā*]

(*lit.*, service) Selfless service; work offered to God, performed without attachment and with the attitude that one is not the doer. In Siddha Yoga meditation ashrams, seva is a spiritual practice, and students seek to perform all of their tasks in this spirit of selfless offering.

SEVITE

One who performs seva.

SHAKTI [*śakti*]

Dynamic spiritual energy; the creative force of God. *See also* KUNDALINI.

SHAKTIPAT [*śaktipāta*]

(*lit.*, descent of grace) Yogic initiation in which the Siddha Guru transmits his spiritual energy into the aspirant, thereby awakening the aspirant's dormant *kundalinī*. *See also* GURU; KUNDALINI.

SHIVA [*śiva*]

1) A name for the one supreme Reality.
2) One of the Hindu trinity of gods, representing God as the destroyer; often understood by yogis as the destroyer of barriers to one's identification with the supreme Self.

SIDDHA [*siddha*]

A fulfilled yogi; one who lives in the state of unity-consciousness; one whose experience of the supreme Self is uninterrupted and whose identification with the ego has been dissolved.

SIDDHALOKA [*siddhaloka*]

(*lit.*, the world of the fulfilled beings) A subtle realm, sometimes experienced in meditation, in which the great Siddha Masters dwell in perpetual bliss. Swami Muktananda described his experience of Siddhaloka in his book *Play of Consciousness*.

SIDDHA YOGA MEDITATION

(*lit.*, the yoga of fulfillment) A path to union of the individual and the divine that begins with shaktipat, the inner awakening by the grace of a Siddha Guru. Siddha Yoga is the name Swami Muktananda gave to this path, which he first brought to the West in 1970;

Swami Chidvilasananda is the living Master of this lineage. *See also* GURU; KUNDALINI; SHAKTIPAT.

SIDDHA YOGA MEDITATION CENTER

A place where people gather to practice Siddha Yoga meditation. There are over 600 Siddha Yoga meditation centers around the world.

SWAMI [*svāmi*]

A respectful term of address for a *sannyāsi*, or monk.

TEMPLE

Unless otherwise specified, "the Temple" refers to the Bhagawan Nityananda Temple in Shree Muktananda Ashram or in Gurudev Siddha Peeth.

VASISHTHA

The legendary sage and Guru of Lord Rama, who epitomized the force of spiritual knowledge. He is the central figure of the *Yoga Vāsishtha*, one of the most rigorous scriptures on the nature of the mind and the way to free it from illusion.

VEDAS [*veda*]

(*lit.*, knowledge) Among the most ancient, revered, and sacred of the world's scriptures, the four Vedas are regarded as divinely revealed, eternal wisdom. They are the *Rig Veda, Atharva Veda, Sāma Veda,* and *Yajur Veda*.

VISHVAMITRA

A brahmin and seer who is said to be the primary author of the *Rig Veda*.

YAJNA [*yajña*]

1) A sacrificial fire ritual in which Vedic mantras are recited while different woods, grains, fruits, oils, yogurt, and ghee (clarified butter) are poured into the fire as offerings to the Lord. 2) Any work or spiritual practice that is offered as worship to God.

Index

GURUMAYI CHIDVILASANANDA

About Gurumayi Chidvilasananda

Gurumayi Chidvilasananda is a spiritual teacher in the ancient yogic tradition of India. As the head of a lineage of meditation Masters, she continues the time-honored role of sages in every tradition—helping seekers awaken to their own inner greatness and to the divinity inherent in the universe. Gurumayi follows in the footsteps of her spiritual Master, Swami Muktananda, who brought the teachings and practices of the path of Siddha Yoga meditation to the West in the 1970s, in what he called a "meditation revolution." Before he passed away in 1982, he selected Gurumayi as his successor and ordained her as a swami, a monk in the Saraswati order. Swami Muktananda was himself the successor to Bhagawan Nityananda, a much-revered saint of modern India.

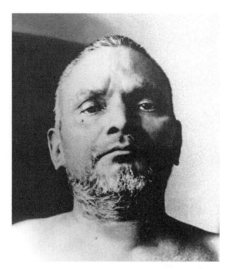

BHAGAWAN NITYANANDA

SWAMI MUKTANANDA

Gurumayi travels widely, taking the teachings and practices of this path to seekers in many countries. She has conducted thousands of programs in cities around the world, as well as in the two major retreat centers of Siddha Yoga meditation: Shree Muktananda Ashram in South Fallsburg, New York, and Gurudev Siddha Peeth in Ganeshpuri, Maharashtra, India.

Gurumayi's work encompasses a charitable organization, The PRASAD Project, that assists people in need in several countries with medical, dental, and community self-help projects.

Wherever she travels, whatever form her work takes, her focus remains the same. Gurumayi calls on people everywhere to wake up to their inner strength and to put into action the natural joy that abounds in their hearts. "The light of the truth is infinite," says Gurumayi, "and this infinite light must definitely be translated into everyday life."

Further Reading

―――⟨◉⟩―――

Published by SYDA Foundation

ENTHUSIASM
Swami Chidvilasananda

"Be filled with enthusiasm and sing God's glory" is the theme of this collection of talks given by Gurumayi Chidvilasananda. In these pages, she inspires us to let the radiance of enthusiasm shine through every action, every thought, every minute of our lives. This, Gurumayi says, is singing God's glory.

THE YOGA OF DISCIPLINE
Swami Chidvilasananda

"From the standpoint of the spiritual path," Gurumayi says, "the term *discipline* is alive with the joyful expectancy of divine fulfillment." In this series of talks on practicing and cultivating discipline of the senses, Gurumayi shows us how this practice brings great joy.

MY LORD LOVES A PURE HEART ~ The Yoga of Divine Virtues
Swami Chidvilasananda

Fearlessness, reverence, compassion, freedom from anger — Gurumayi describes how these magnificent virtues are an integral part of our true nature. This is a revealing commentary on chapter 16 of the *Bhagavad Gītā*.

THE MAGIC OF THE HEART ~ Reflections on Divine Love
Swami Chidvilasananda

In these profound and tender reflections on divine love, Gurumayi makes it clear that the supreme Heart is a place we must get to know. It is here, she tells us, in the interior of the soul, that "the Lord reveals Himself every second of the day."

PLAY OF CONSCIOUSNESS
Swami Muktananda

In this intimate and powerful autobiography, Swami Muktananda, Gurumayi's Guru, describes his own journey to Self-realization, revealing the process of transformation he experienced under the guidance of his Guru, Bhagawan Nityananda.

FROM THE FINITE TO THE INFINITE
Swami Muktananda

This compilation of questions and answers is drawn from Baba Muktananda's travels in the West. In it, Baba addresses all the issues a seeker might encounter on the spiritual path, from the earliest days until the culmination of the journey.

RESONATE WITH STILLNESS ~ Daily Contemplations
Swami Muktananda, Swami Chidvilasananda

Every sentence of this exquisite collection of contemplations is an expression of wisdom and love from the Siddha Masters Baba Muktananda and Gurumayi Chidvilasananda. The selections are arranged in twelve themes of spiritual life, with a contemplation for each day of the year.

You may learn more about the teachings and
practices of Siddha Yoga meditation by contacting

SYDA Foundation
P.O. Box 600
371 Brickman Rd.
South Fallsburg, NY 12779-0600, USA
Tel: 914-434-2000

or

Gurudev Siddha Peeth
P.O. Ganeshpuri
PIN 401 206
District Thana
Maharashtra, India

For further information on books in print by
Swami Muktananda and Swami Chidvilasananda, editions in translation,
and audio and video recordings, please contact

Siddha Yoga Meditation Bookstore
P.O. Box 600
371 Brickman Rd.
South Fallsburg, NY 12779-0600, USA
Tel: 914-434-2000 ext. 1700

Call toll-free from the United States and Canada: 888-422-3334
Fax toll-free from the United States and Canada: 888-422-3339